There once was a child with a big, bold dream,
To preach like his Pastor, or so it would seem!

HONOR
The Pastor spoke strong, with passion and might,
And Little Saint thought, "I'll honor God with my life!"
With respect and care, he'd do his best,
To serve God anywhere, passing each test.

Little Saint carried his Pastor's Bible and water,
Following closely, never to falter.
"Honor means showing love and respect.
In all I do, God's path I'll protect."

EXCELLENCE
"Anywhere, anytime, I'll give my best,
Serving with excellence, passing the test."
It's not about having the best of things,
But doing your best in everything.

He helped in the parking, greeted with smiles,
And walked to serve, covering many miles.
With excellence shining in all that he did,
Doing his best was all God asked.

COURAGE
As he grew, he served as an usher with the youth.
When challenges came, he stood strong in truth.
Trusting in God, always in prayer,
Believing that God was always there.

Courage is faith when times get tough,
Trusting in God when life feels rough.
Little Saint knew God's strength was real,
To stand tall no matter how he'd feel.

SACRIFICE
As an adult, he served in the nursery and kids' rooms.
He worked with a grin, through all of the rooms.
Teaching the children, helping them see,
That serving with kids was the place to be!
Week in and week out, he served with his all.
Because this was part of his heavenly call.

Sacrifice means giving without looking back.
For serving God, there's nothing you lack.
Little Saint put others first every day,
Knowing God's work would always stay.

UNITY
He led young adults, showing he cared.
With love and kindness, God's truth was shared.
In unity, they served as one.
Together in faith, God's work was done.

As Little Saint grew, his dream stayed strong,
Though preaching hadn't yet come along.
But he served with faith, year after year,
Trusting God's plan, always near.

"If preaching won't happen, that's just fine. Serving God's work is truly divine."

Now at thirty-six, his heart full of grace,
Little Saint kept running God's race.
He led and taught with wisdom and care,
Bringing joy to the church everywhere.

Then one fine day, came a surprise.
"Will you be a pastor?" filled Little Saint's eyes!

A dream thought lost was now alive.
God had watched as Little Saint strived.

So if you wonder, "Will my dreams come true?"
Just remember, God's waiting on you!

Little Saint served with a smile so bright,
Knowing God saw his heart as just right.

And though he felt late to his dream,
He trusted God and answered the call, it would seem.

So dream again, let your faith grow.
With God by your side, His plans you'll know!

"Anywhere, anytime, for God you will go,
And just like Little Saint, His path you'll follow!"

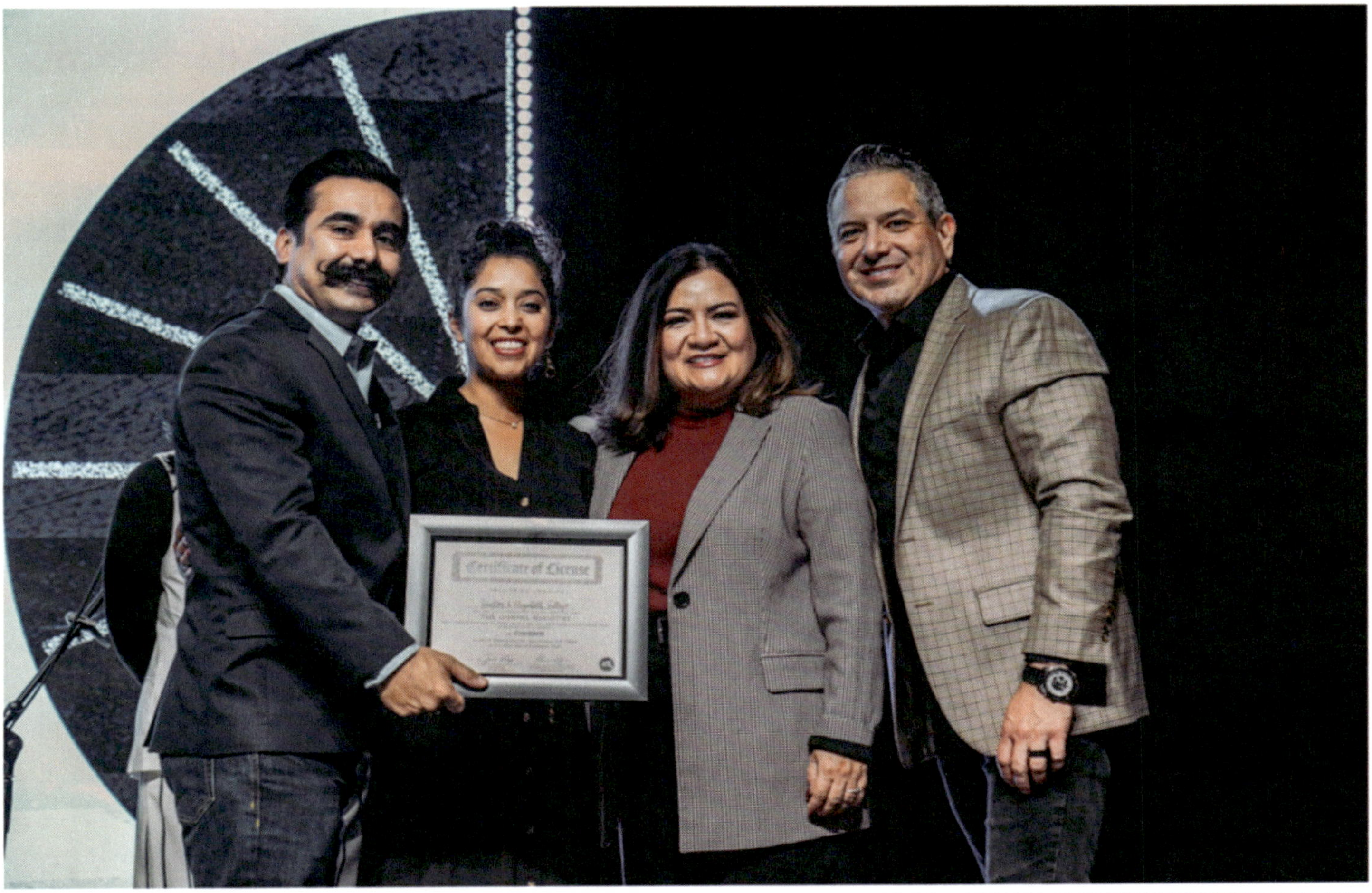
Certificate of License

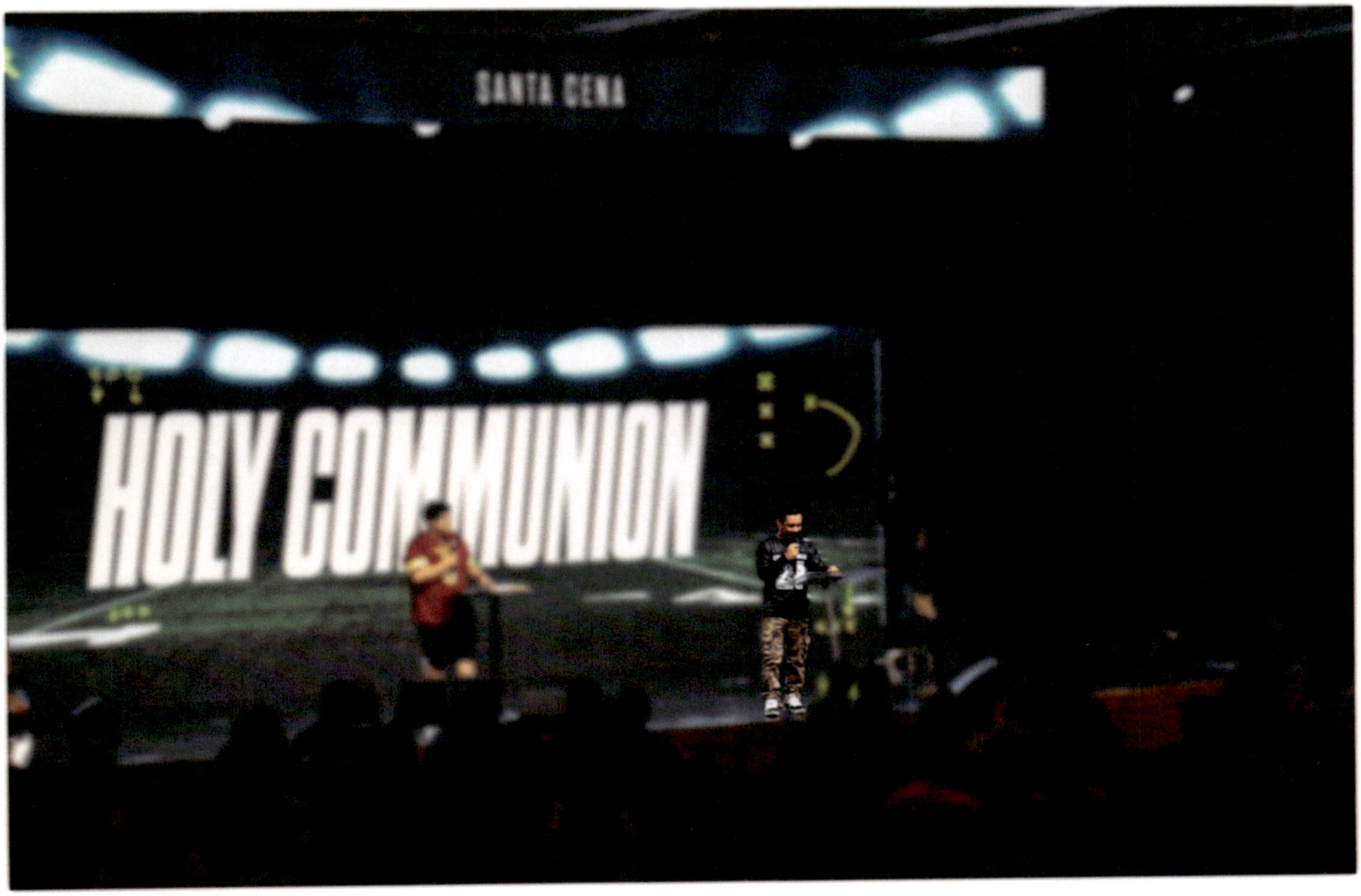
SANTA CENA
HOLY COMMUNION